THE INDIAN STREET FOOD

A CULTURAL AND GASTRONOMIC EXPLORATION OF INDIA'S STREET FOOD

DR. JAGADEESH PILLAI

Made with ♥ on the Notion Press Platform
www.notionpress.com

|| "Dedicated to all who seek to understand and appreciate Indian culture and tradition." ||

ꕥ

Contents

Contents

PRAYER

"Om Bhadram Karnebhih Shrunuyaama DevaahBhadram Pashyemaakshabhiryajatraah Sthirairangaistushtuvaamsastanoobhih Vyashema Devahitam YadaayuhSwasti Na Indro VridhashravaahSwasti Nah Pooshaa VishwavedaahSwasti Nastaarkshyo ArishtanemihSwasti No Brihaspatir DadhaatuOm Shantih, Shantih, Shantih"

The literal meaning of this mantra is: OM. O Gods! Let us hear auspicious words from our ears. O reverent Gods! Let us behold propitious visions from our eyes, let our organs and body be stable, healthy, and strong. Let us do that which is pleasing to the gods in the life span allotted to us. May Indra, inscribed in the scriptures, bring us fortune! May Pushan, the knower of the world, grant us prosperity! May Trakshya, who vanquishes enemies, bestow us with blessings! May Brihaspati bring us success!
OM Peace, Peace, Peace.

About The Author

Dr. Jagadeesh Pillai is a renowned Guinness World Record holder, writer, and researcher hailing from Varanasi, also known as the abode of Lord Shiva. With a Ph.D. in Vedic Science and a range of creative ideas and achievements, he is a true polymath. He is the author of more than 100 books including Research Publications. Although his roots can be traced back to Kerala, the people of Varanasi hold him in high regard and affectionately consider him one of their own.

Dr. Pillai has achieved four Guinness World Records in the following subjects:

"Script to Screen" - In this record, Dr. Pillai produced and directed an animation film within the shortest time possible, breaking the previous record set by Canadians. He has also received numerous national and international awards and recognitions for this achievement.

Longest Line of Postcards - For this record, Dr. Pillai created a line of 16,300 postcards on the occasion of the 163rd anniversary of Indian Postal Day. The event also included a questionnaire about the Indian flag.

Largest Poster Awareness Campaign - Dr. Pillai designed an awareness campaign on the subject of "Beti Bachao - Beti Padhao" (Save the Girl Child - Educate the Girl Child) to achieve this record.

Largest Envelope - In tribute to the Indian Prime Minister's

"Make in India" initiative, Dr. Pillai created a 4000 square meter envelope using waste paper to achieve this record.

Attempted - **70000 Candles on a 210 kg Cake** - To celebrate the 70th Indian Independence Day, Dr. Pillai attempted to light 70,000 candles on a 210 kg cake, which was recorded in World Records India.

Attempted - **Documentary on Dhamek Stupa of Sarnath in 17 Languages** - Dr. Pillai attempted to create a documentary on the Dhamek Stupa of Sarnath, dubbing it in 17 different languages. The result of this attempt is currently awaiting confirmation from the Guinness World Records.

Dr. Pillai is skilled in teaching the Bhagavad Gita, a Hindu scripture, and is popular among young people. He has helped many young people improve their lives through his motivational teachings.

In addition to teaching, he has composed and sung numerous Sanskrit Bhajans and patriotic songs.

He has also written and directed several short films and documentaries for awareness campaigns, and has volunteered with the police in both UP and Kerala to spread awareness about various issues through videos and photography.

Incredibly, he has produced and directed over 100 documentaries about the city of Varanasi, all on his own.

He has also helped and guided more than 25 boys and girls to achieve world records through creative and innovative methods. He is a multifaceted person who uses his intellect and the blessings given to him by God to excel in various areas. He is both a teacher and a student, always learning and teaching, and is able to master any subject he comes across.

He is a selfless social activist and motivational speaker who has overcome struggles and failures to become a successful and enthusiastic individual with a rich life experience.

In addition to his work with the Bhagavad Gita, he is also an efficient Tarot card reader, Astro-Vastu consultant, and a talented singer and composer. He has sung the entire Ram Charita Manas and Bhagavad Gita in his own compositions, and has sung the phrase "Lokah Samastha Sukhino Bhavantu" in 50 different languages. He is currently working on a detailed and scientific study of Vedas, Upanishads, Puranas, and the Bhagavad Gita. He has also composed and sung the Hanuman Chalisa and Gayatri Mantra in 108 and 1008 different compositions, respectively.

Awards - Four Times Guinness World Records, Winner of Mahatma Gandhi Vishwa Shanti Puraskar, Mahatma Gandhi Global Peace Ambassador, Kashi Ratna Award, Dr. APJ Abdul Kalam Motivational Person of the Year 2017, Mother Teresa Award, Indira Gandhi Priyadarshini Award, Bharat Vikas Ratna Award, Udyog Ratna Award, Vigyan Prasar Award, Poorvanchal Ratn Samman.

PREFACE

Indian street food is an integral part of the country's culture, history, and economy. From puchkas to kathi rolls to paan and jalebi, every turn leads to something new and delicious to tantalize both the eyes and the taste buds. This book, The Indian Street Food: A Cultural and Gastronomic Exploration of India's Street Food, seeks to explore the culture, history, and significance of Indian street food.

This book is intended to serve as an introduction to the rich history and culture of Indian street food for readers who are new to the subject. It explores the origins of Indian street food, the regional variations in street food, and popular street foods of India. It also examines the spice of street food in India, the health implications of eating street food, the economic importance of street food, the growing popularity of street food, the culture of eating street food, and the future of Indian street food.

The book draws on research from a variety of sources, including interviews with key figures in the Indian street food industry, archival materials, and cultural analysis. I have also conducted extensive field research in India, including attending street food festivals, interviewing street food vendors, and visiting locations associated with the production of street food. Through this research, I hope to provide readers with a comprehensive understanding of the Indian street food industry and its various components.

I am deeply passionate about the art of Indian street food and hope that this book will help to spread the appreciation of this wonderful form of cuisine. I believe that Indian street food has a great deal to offer to the world and I am excited to share its cultural and historical significance with my readers.

I

Indian street food is a unique and vibrant culinary experience, filled with cultural and gastronomic exploration. For centuries, Indians have been creating a tantalizing array of small street eats that have become integral to Indian culture and embody the cuisine's culinary ingenuity. From the spice-filled chaat corners of Mumbai to the bhelpuri stands of Kolkata, the streets of India remain alive with activity and flavor, boasting an abundance of street food to explore.

For tourists and locals alike, Indian street food offers a rich and enjoyable gastronomic experience. Whether standing in line for a savory samosa or tucking into warm pau bhaji, the flavors and aromas of Indian street food are simply irresistible. Traditional selections like kulcha-chole, pav bhaji, momos, and golgappas are not only delicious but provide a unique glimpse into the diverse culinary culture of India.

The variations of flavors and textures in Indian street food are an indication of its abundant cultural heritage. Each region boasts a different style of cooking, reflecting the communal and regional preferences of its people. Popular dishes like vada pav or biryani in Southern India display the region's fondness for flavorful spices, while the tikkis and chaats in Northern India showcase the region's specialties of tangy chutneys and savory potatoes. Every bite of Indian street food is a reflection of the country's centuries-old culinary customs.

Of course, no exploration of Indian street food would be complete without a traditional drink. Indian chai tea is the perfect accompaniment to any street food dish, lending its bright, smoky flavors to the already delicious selection of items. A sip of mint-flavored lassi is a perfect pick-me-up after a flavorful meal.

From the bustling cities of Delhi to the peaceful mountain foothills of Uttar Pradesh, Indian street food remains a showcase of local culture and cuisine. Generations of cooks have crafted an array of traditional dishes, taking the country's cuisine to new heights and delighting taste buds around the nation. With a wide variety of dishes to try and flavors to explore, Indian street food is truly a unique and delicious culinary experience.

"Indian food is always an adventure. Every bite is a flavor explosion."

-Rashmi Primlani

II

The History of Indian Street Food

The centuries-old legacy of Indian street food has both tantalized and charmed its admirers for generations. A salivating concoction of flavors and spices, this beloved cuisine has its roots planted firmly in India's diverse cultural and historical background. With a seemingly endless variety of savory treats, this type of food has long-since inspired modern adaptations for both home and restaurant kitchens.

The origins of Indian street food stretch back thousands of years, when travelers from around the world gathered at local markets to purchase items from across the Subcontinent. Early recipes developed from combinations of regional ingredients, like lentils, veggies and native herbs and spices, which were often fried on a flat griddle to create tasty snacks.

Over time, more inventive food vendors began to spring up in the bustling cities of India, serving everything from hot samosas to flavorful kachoris. Notable examples of street food in India include chaats, an umbrella term for all savory snacks, as well as pani puri, deep-fried flour puffs filled with vegetable dishes, and vada pav, a Mumbai specialty comprised of a spicy potato patty served in a bread bun.

Indian street food also has historical connections to the nation's caste system. In some regions, certain citizens and laborers were only allowed to frequent street food vendors, or even prohibited from consuming freshly cooked food. These restrictions increased the popularity of street food, which gradually spread across India and other parts of the world, particularly within the South Asian diaspora.

Today, street food remains a vital part of India's gastronomic identity, especially in cities like Mumbai and Chennai. Local businesses still serve up snacks, such as burfi, jalebis and chai tea, each with their own distinct and delicious flavors. The country also boasts its own Street Food Festival each year, providing a vibrant and colorful display of the stunning variety of street food on offer.

Throughout its lengthy history, Indian street food has remained a source of joy, comfort and pride for its appreciative fan base. No matter where or when it's enjoyed, this fare continues to tantalize the taste buds of locals and tourists alike. Whether found at a bustling marketplace or recreated in a home kitchen, Indian street food will always stand out as one of India's most revered cuisines.

"Food is an integral part of Indian culture, where eating spicy dishes is a way of life."

-Deepak Menon

ꕥ

III

Regional Variations in Street Food

India is home to a variety of splendid mouth-watering dishes, including a large spectrum of delicious street food. Across the large subcontinent, regional variations of the same type of food can be found, each specific to the area and embodying the culture that has arisen from local and historical influences. Indian street food is known to be full of flavor and variety, with numerous unique and delicious options that have been developed through exposure to different cultures and customs.

The street food varies greatly between North India, South India, West India, and East India. Northern Indian-style street food is full of flavor and utilizes a variety of spices that are distinctive to the area, such as coriander, cumin, garam masala, and red chili powder. In North India, street food is often served with breads like chapati, naan, and paratha. Dishes like butter paneer, channa bhatura, and tikka are common. Street food like Chaat in Old Delhi has become extremely popular as a snack and meal.

In the South, rice is the staple in the diet, so most of the street food is prepared with it. Famous dishes like dosa, idli, vada, and uttapam are served with sambar and chutney. Samosa, chana bhaji, and curd rice are other popular options. Biryani is another favorite, with its huge variety of flavors and its ability to please many different palate types.

The street food in West India is a reflection of the area's mix of cultures and regions, with recipes native to the state, as well as those brought in by people from other states. Dishes like misal pav, bhelpuri, vada pav, and pav bhaji have become extremely popular. The street food in West India is also heavily influenced by its coastal areas, with an abundance of seafood dishes as well.

In East India, street food is full of flavor and usually contains some kind of fish or seafood. Dishes like pihi, bhaja, muri, and ghugni are common on street corners. Specialties like Cuisine Martab can be seen in markets and haats. Thukpa, a traditional Tibetan dish, is also a favorite of the region.

The street food of India is incredibly varied and delicious. Each region has developed its own unique and distinct style of food, which is a reflection of its culture, customs, and historical influences. As India continues to introduce new dishes, the street food of this magnificent country will continue to evolve and become even more varied and delicious.

"Indian food is special because it is a combination of multiple flavors. The spices are intense and unique. "

-Ashley Jacob

ꕥ

IV

Popular Street Foods of India

India is a country with a long history of street food tradition, and it is a major part of the culture and cuisine in the country. Every corner of India is a feast when it comes to savoring the diverse flavors of its street food. From chaat,to pani puri,to samosa, Indian street food has made its way worldwide, providing a tantalizing glimpse of traditional Indian flavors.

Chaat, one of the most popular street foods in India, is an Indian savory snack made from a combination of spicy, tangy and sweet ingredients. This popular snack can be found almost anywhere in India. It is typically made with crunchy fried dough called puri, boiled potatoes, chutney, assorted vegetables, yogurt and tamarind-date chutney. Chaat is served both as a light meal or a snack.

Another popular Indian street food is pani puri, also known

as golgappas. It is a type of deep fried ball made with a wheat flour and semolina dough, stuffed with some spicy potatoes, flavored water called pani, chopped onion, tomato and coriander. It is commonly served with a sweet and tangy chutney. This dish is highly popular all over India, and is an ideal snack in the hot summer months.

Then there is samosa, an Indian snack made of several wheat flour dough encasing a tasty filling of potatoes, onions and spices. This simple snack is an all time favorite of people all over India, and is a regular fixture of wedding receptions and other celebrations. Samosas are usually served with a chutney or a dipping sauce.

Finally, for those who prefer something sweet, jalebi is the perfect street food. This delicious dessert is made from a batter of refined flour, yogurt and sugar. It is deep-fried in oil, then soaked in a sugar syrup. Jalebi is typically served hot with a side of thickened milk, or rabdi for some extra sweetness.

These are just some of the most popular street foods of India. From chaat,to pani puri,to samosa, Indian street food is not only a mouth-watering delicacy but also provides a window into the vibrant culture of the country. Street food is an integral part of the Indian culinary customs, and a must-try experience of any traveler exploring India.

"The joy of Indian food comes from the combination of sweet, sour, salty, spicy, and pungent ingredients used in creating amazing dishes."

-Trip Atwood

V

The Spice of Street Food in India

India is a country with a proud street food culture. From the bustling cities to the rural villages, street food is ubiquitous throughout the county. Indian street food is widely known for its authentic and flavorful spices, making it a favorite among tourists and locals alike.

Street food often takes the form of small-scale, casual eateries such as chaat stands, dhabas, mobile carts, and even the occasional pavement vendor. It is an affordable, convenient, and tasty way for Indian citizens to quickly satisfy their hunger without having to invest in a full-fledged meal. Street food is a great way to enjoy the distinct aromas and flavors of Indian cuisine.

Indian street food commonly contains a variety of spices, herbs, and seasonings. These spices are key to why street food is so flavorful. Most dishes contain a combination of one or more of the spices: cumin, chili, turmeric, and coriander. The classic chaat dish, for example, contains a combination of these spices mixed with onions, tomatoes, green chilies, and fresh cilantro. Other common Indian spices used in street food include ginger, garlic, mustard, fennel, asafetida, fenugreek, black pepper, and cumin. The use of these spices provides a unique and delicious flavor to Indian street food.

Spicy foods are a central theme in Indian cuisine. Street food is no exception, with tantalizing spicy dishes such as tandoori chicken, vada pav, and pav bhaji. These dishes are often heavily spiced and seasoned, providing a tingly sensation on the tongue and a fragrant aroma in the air. The layers of spices used in street food create a complex and savory flavor, making it a beloved part of the Indian food culture.

Indian street food is appreciated throughout the country and the world for its unique and highly spiced flavors. Whether it's the classic chaat dish, tandoori chicken, or vada pav, Indian street food always packs a punch. The combination of herbs and spices used in street food give it its distinctive flavor, making it a refreshing and satisfying food experience.

"Vegetables, grains, and spices are staples of Indian cuisine. Each one adds flavor, color, and nutrition to the meal."

-Sanjay Kumar

ℬ

VI

Street Food and Health

India is renowned for its street food and has long been a place to enjoy flavorful snacks and meals, as well as entertaining environment of being able to watch the food being made. India has an incredibly diverse range of street vendors, offering a huge variety of dishes from different parts of the country, such as chaat, dosas, idlis, vada pav, kathi rolls, pani puri and of course many types of tandoori. With its unique cooking style, beautiful accompaniments, and mind blowing aromas, it's no wonder why Indian street food has been growing in popularity, even across the globe.

However, while Indian Street Food is popular and tasty, there is also a great deal of concern regarding its potential health risks because of issues such as hygiene and the oil used in the food preparation. This is because the standards of hygiene in some street food vendors can be extremely different from those in a more established restaurant, as they are usually not subject to the same quality control. The utensils they use may also not be cleaned properly, and the water they use to clean them may not be of the best quality.

Another potential health risk is the oil used to fry the food. Many street food vendors use large quantities of oil for deep frying, which can contain high levels of saturated fats. Saturated fats can be detrimental to our health in the long term as they can increase cholesterol levels, contributing to a range of cardiovascular diseases. Furthermore, the oil may not be changed regularly, which leads to further deterioration of the quality.

Therefore, it is important to be aware of the health risks associated with eating Indian Street Food and to take measures to ensure it is safe for consumption. One of the most important precautions to take is to choose hygienic vendors, such as those operating in more established spots, rather than back-street ones. In addition, you can look out for whether the vendors are taking safety measures such as using clean utensils and changing the oil regularly.

Overall, as long as Indian Street Food is enjoyed in moderation and from hygienic sources, it can be part of a balanced diet and a wonderful way to appreciate India's incredible food culture.

However, it is always important to remember that street food poses certain risks that can't be taken lightly and to be vigilant in checking the quality of the food before eating.

"Aromatic herbal concoctions and spice combinations define Indian cuisine and bring life to any meal. "

-Shyamal Patel

ఐ

VII

Street Food and Economy

In India, street food is more than just a tasty snack. It is an expensive and integral part of the Indian economy and culture. Traditionally, street food has been prepared in the open air and then sold to customers in the streets, most commonly in front of retail stores.

India is home to some of the most unique and delicious street foods in the world. From simple snack items such as samosas, pakoras, and bhajiyas to full meals such as pav bhaji, aloo chaat, and dosa, Indian street food consists of a vast variety of food items. Street food vendors in India prepare these snacks from fresh ingredients and serve them hot in order to maintain their quality. The street food vendors are a vital part of the local economy and provide employment to millions of people from diverse communities and economic backgrounds.

Street food vendors in India generate a large amount of income for the local community. The sale of street food is highly competitive and requires hustle and ingenuity. The vendors set up shop in busy areas and use creative promotions such as discounted pricing and vibrant displays to attract customers. The sale of street food also generates a large number of indirect jobs in the form of cleaners, helpers, and suppliers. In addition, the sale of street food provides numerous benefits to the local economy including employment, skill development, and income generation.

Despite the many benefits of street food, there are some drawbacks as well. The street food industry is largely unorganized and devoid of regulations. This leads to lack of safety standards and poor hygiene at many street food stalls, which may lead to health hazards. In addition, the vendors often work long hours and receive low wages, leading to low levels of job satisfaction. There is also an environmental component to consider, as street food vendors often rely on the burning of coal or wood which results in air pollution.

Thus, street food is a vital part of the Indian economy and culture. It helps to generate income through job creation, skill development and income generation. However, there are also some drawbacks to street food that need to be addressed in order to ensure its sustainability. Regulations need to be enforced to ensure safety standards, and there should be measures taken to minimize the environmental impact of street food vendors. With the right policies and initiatives, street food can continue to be a vibrant part of the Indian economy and culture.

"Indian food is the combination of complex flavors and intricate preparations, making it unique and delicious. "

-Mona Mathur

ꕤ

VIII

The Growing Popularity of Street Food

The growing popularity of Indian Street Food can be attributed to the refinement of the dishes and the blending of global tastes and flavors, creating an interesting cultural experience for those who indulge in it.

The first Indian street food appeared in India over five thousand years ago, as travelers and traders would congregate in busy bazaars to sample the local delicacies. This tradition continues today as more and more people discover the culinary delights of India and its often colorful street food scene. Indian street food is a reflection of the country's colorful diversity and culture.

Indian street food has been a hallmark of the Indian food scene since time immemorial, and it is only continuing to gain more popularity with passing time. The growing popularity of Indian street food can be mainly attributed to the delicious tastes and flavors found within the dishes. The savory flavors and aromas created by the seasonings used are a far cry from the bland spicelessness of many western dishes. Furthermore, Indian recipes often involve the blending of multiple spices, which in turn creates a range of flavors to suit any palette. Indian street food is a tour de force of tastes, fragrances and aromas.

The most popular Indian street food item today is undoubtedly the street food tikka masala. Tikka masala has become a staple in many global restaurants and takeaways, as well as Indian street food vendors throughout the country. This dish is a combination of marinated boneless hot meat, onions, tomatoes and special masala which is cooked in a curry or tomato-based sauce. Due to its popularity, tikka masala is becoming increasingly available in various regions around the world.

In addition to tikka masala, other popular Indian street food items include Dosa, an Indian pancake; Chola batura, a deep-fried bread filled with potatoes; Pav Bhaji, an Indian burger; as well as many other snack items such as samosas, aloo tikki, and pani puri. All these items are commonly found in Indian street food outlets and are especially popular amongst Indian children and teenagers. As such, Indian street food is extremely popular amongst young people and with tourists and visitors to the country.

The growing popularity of Indian street food is a reflection of the refinement of the dishes and the blending of global flavors. The most popular items are tikka masala, dosa, and chola batura, as well as many other snack items such as samosas, aloo tikki, and pani puri. The delicious tastes, fragrances and aromas, as well as the cultural experience it provides, make Indian street food a delightful meal for those who are lucky enough to try it.

"Indian food is the perfect party food, as it allows guests to taste a variety of flavors and textures at the same time."

-Viraj Sharma

ꕥ

IX

The Culture of Eating Street Food

The regional culture of eating street food in India is hard to ignore. Street food vendors hawking their wares on the side of the roads and in crowded city centers comprising of the subcontinent's rich and vibrant cuisine have long been an integral part of the local culture. In different cities and towns across India, there are unique snacks, desserts, and meals that would be hard to find anywhere else.

Pointing to the variety of regional Indian street food is difficult since it's so vast and different from place to place. However, there are a few generic dishes like samosas and chaat that can be found throughout India. Samosas are fried turnovers with a spicy filling, and chaat is a mix of mashed potatoes or legumes, yogurt, and various garnishes. These dishes have become immensely popular even in western countries and feature prominently in the Indian street food culture.

In the southern state of Kerala, the traditional street food is dominated by a mix of Indian, Portuguese, and Dutch flavors. This can be seen in dishes like appam and stew, which consists of a dosa-like pancake filled with coconut filling, and stewed vegetables, rice, and meats. Then there is the coastal staple, dhuska, which is a deep fried snack made with rice, lentils, and onion.

Moving up to the north, the cuisine becomes more meat-based and with the strong flavor of garam masala, the popular spice blend of India. Naan, the most common flatbread here, is a staple in the region and can be served with a variety of comforting curries. Kulfi, a popular winter snack, is also characterized by spices like cardamom, saffron, and mace, which come together to create a delicately sweet and creamy experience.

Throughout India, street food is an important part of both culture and cuisine. Not only is it accessible and affordable to eat, but it also offers an insight into the traditional dishes of India. Through street food, one can get a glimpse into the culture and lifestyles of the people in India, as well as the unique flavors found in each region. From the flavored desserts of Kerala to the famed samosas of Delhi, Indian street food offers a unique and delicious experience for those who try it.

"Indian food has influenced many cultures and continues to inspire creativity in the kitchen all around the world."

-Nirav Jasani

India is famous for its street food cuisine, with an array of vendors to choose from and flavors that tantalize the taste buds. India's street food has always been popular throughout the country, but as Indian cities modernize, the question arises as to what the future of street food in India holds.

Indian cities are growing faster than ever, and this rapid urbanization is resulting in an increased demand for food that can be cooked quickly and at a low cost. With this demand in mind, Indian cities are welcoming more street food vendors than ever before in order to meet the needs of their citizens. This increased popularity of street food reflects the country's love of convenience and cheap food that can be enjoyed on the go.

Another factor driving the future of Indian street food is the trend towards healthier meals. As levels of health awareness increases, customers are now looking for more health-conscious food choices. In response to this, more vendors are offering healthier options that are low in fat, high in fiber, and free from preservatives. In addition, many street food vendors are utilizing local ingredients, utilizing eco-friendly cooking methods, and making efforts to reduce their environmental footprint.

The ubiquity of the Internet has also played a part in the future of Indian street food. As more vendors go online, customers are now able to order their favorite meals through digital delivery services. In addition to making ordering street food easier, this has also opened up avenues for experimentation and innovation, as vendors are now able to offer a variety of new flavors and dishes.

The future of Indian street food looks bright. As cities modernize and people look for healthier options, street food vendors are responding to that demand by providing customers with healthier options and utilizing modern technologies such as online delivery services. The future of Indian street food is one of innovations and experimentation, ensuring that customers can always find the perfect meal on the street.

"Indian food is tasty and healthy. It appeals to all tastes and dietary needs."

-Rachana Chokshi

❧

XI

Experiencing Indian Street Food

Indian street food is a beloved culinary tradition that many people around the world enjoy experiencing. Street food vendors often take pride in the inventive snacks they are able to make with simple ingredients. From the tantalizing smell of chaat and bhel puri in Mumbai to the juicy flavors of kebabs in Delhi, Indian street food is an incredible part of the culture and the experience of India.

One of the most popular Indian street food snacks is bhel puri. It is a popular roadside snack in Mumbai which is a mixture of puffed rice, boiled potatoes, onions, spicy chutneys, and some other condiments. It is much loved for its creamy and tangy flavors and is often eaten as a snack throughout the day.

Another popular Indian street food snack is sev puri. It is a small, crisp pancake made from semolina and other ingredients such as onions, potatoes, and chutneys. It is usually eaten as a quick snack in between meals and enjoyed for the spiciness and the crunchy texture.

Kebabs are another popular Indian street food. Durban-style seekh kebabs, for example, are made from seasoned minced lamb that is spiced with ginger, garlic, and cumin. Traditionally, these kebabs are served on toasty laffa bread loaded with rich condiments and are usually a great hit with locals and tourists alike.

If one is adventurous enough, they may even try some unique Indian street food such as Guntur-style chilli chicken. It is a boneless fried chicken with a spicy, chili-based sauce that is full of flavor. This dish is a specialty of Guntur in Andhra Pradesh and is popular in local restaurants.

In addition to the savory snacks, Indian street food is also famous for its sweet treats. Jalebi is one such treat which is small, spiral-shaped sweet pretzels made with all-purpose flour, sugar, and saffron syrup. It is usually served hot and is often eaten with a scoop of creamy ice cream for a truly decadent treat.

Indian street food is a great experience for those looking to try new and unusual cuisines. It is definitely a great way to try the flavors of India from the comfort of the streets, as there are a variety of snacks and treats to satisfy everyone's palate. Not only is it cheap and delicious, but it is also a great way to explore Indian culture and experience the charms of India.

"The use of spices and herbs in Indian cooking adds wonderful flavors to the dishes, for a truly memorable experience."

-Avi Bhavsar

ജ

Other Books Of The Author

1. The Moments When I Met God
2. Kashiyile Theertha Pathangal
3. GURU GYAN VANI
4. Abhiprerak Gita
5. ASSI SE JAIN GHAT TAK
6. Hopelessness of Arjuna
7. The Soul and It's True Nature
8. Sense of Action (Karma)
9. Action through Wisdom
10. Action through Wisdom
11. THEORY AND PRACTICAL OF EVERY ACTION
12. LOGICAL UNDERSTANDING OF THE SUPREME
13. THE IMPERISHABLE SUPREME
14. Yatra Nishadraj se Hanuman Ghat Tak
15. Yatra Karnatak Ghat se Raja Ghat Tak
16. Yatra Pandey Ghat se Prayagraj Ghat Tak
17. Yatra Ranjendra Prasad Ghat se Dattatreya Ghat Tak
18. YaatraSindhiya Ghat se Gwaliar Ghat Tak
19. Yatra Mangala Gauri Ghat se Hanuman Gadhi Ghat Tak
20. Yatra Gaay Ghat Se Nishad Ghat Tak
21. MAA GANGA, GHATEN EVM UTSAV
22. Ganga Arti Dev Deepavali evam Any Utsav
23. Potentials of Digitalized India
24. VEDIC CONSCIOUSNESS
25. A Brief Introduction to Vedic Science
26. Kashi ke Barah Jyotirling
27. IMPACT OF MOTIVATION
28. Let's have a Milky Way Journey
29. Color Therapy in a Nutshell

30. Rigveda in a Nutshell
31. Yajurveda in a Nutshell
32. Samveda in a Nutshell
33. Atharva Veda in a Nutshell
34. Ayushman Bhava - Ayurveda
35. Srimad Bhagavad Gita and Upanishad Connection
36. Srimad Bhagavad Gita - an attempt to summarize each chapter.
37. Facts and Impact of Nakshatra
38. Astro Gems - NAVARATNA
39. Ekadashi - A Concise Overview
40. A Concise View of Hanuman Chalisa
41. Inspirational Gita
42. Nakshatraranyam
43. Summary of 18 Mahapuranas
44. Synopsis of 18 Upa Puranas
45. Rigvediya Upanishads
46. Shukla Yajurvediya Upanishads
47. Krishna Yajurvediya Upanishads
48. Samavediya Upanishads
49. Atharvavediya Upanishads
50. The Seven Great Sages
51. From Rocket Scientist to President Dr. APJ Abdul Kalam
52. The Visionary's Voice - Quotes of Dr. APJ Abdul Kalam
53. The Wisdom of Swami Vivekananda: Insights and Inspiration from a Legendary Spiritual Teacher
54. Ayurvedic Remedies from the Garden
55. Sages and Seers
56. Rising Strong – Motivational Stories of Women
57. Beyond Flames -Mystery stories of Funeral Ghat Manikarnika
58. The Origins of Tulsi: A Look at the Mythological Roots of the Plant"

59. The Holistic Cow: A Look at the Physical, Spiritual, and Cultural Importance of Cows in India
60. Arts of Healing
61. Exploring the Divine
62. Understanding Five Elements
63. The Etymology of Ram
64. Symbols of India
65. Voice of Change (About Speeches of Great Men)
66. She Speaks (About Speeches of Great Women)
67. Patriotism on Celluloid – Brief About Patriotic Films
68. The Music of Motivation: A Brief Guide to Inspirational Film Songs
69. **Unlocking the Secrets of the Dashopanishads**
70. A Cultural Mosaic
71. Ancient Traditions, Modern Minds
72. Ecos of Ancient Wisdom
73. Beneath the Surface
74. From Temples to Ashrams
75. Sages of the Subcontinent
76. The Art of Healling (Ayurveda, Yoga & Naturopathy)
77. Indian Kitchen
78. The Festivals of India
79. The Indian Epics Retold
80. The Power of Mantras
81. The Indian River Ganges
82. The Indian Architecture
83. Rites of Passage
84. The Indian Silk Road
85. The Indian Literature
86. The Indian Villages
87. The Indian Folks & Crafts
88. The Way of Buddha
89. The Ramayan of Tulsidas

90. Astrological Remedies
91. The Secret Power of Motivation
92. Secret of Developing your Inner Strength
93. The Secret Path to Motivation
94. The Art and Secret of Positive Thinking
95. The Secrets of Practicing Ethical Living
96. Indian Art and Painting
97. The Indian Herbalism
98. Bharatanatyam to Kathak
99. Exploring India's Astrological Remedies
100. The Indian Festival of Flowers
101. Indian Handicrafts
102. The Splashes of Joy – India's Colour Festival

CONTACT

DR. JAGADEESH PILLAI

PhD in Vedic Science

Four Times Guinness World Record Holder

Winner of Mahatma Gandhi Vishwa Shanti Puraskar and Global Peace Ambassador

Gemology, Astro & Vastu Consultant - Spiritual Counselor

Consultant for designing World Record Ideas

Efficient Tarot Card Reader

9839093003

myrichindia@gmail.com

drjagadeeshpillai@facebook

drjagadeeshpillai@instagram

jagadeeshpillai@youtube

www. JAGADEESHPILLAI.com

|| LOKAHA SAMASTHAHA SUKHINO BHAVANTU ||

9 798889 517702

Printed by Libri Plureos GmbH in Hamburg,
Germany